"Mary Ann Wehler's *Throat* is an astonishing collection, with a voice of extraordinary purity, taking out of ordinary life our sensational interiors: outgrowing one's family and history, including the gritty history of white working-class insecurities; stories of pain that are also celebrations of deep physical intimacy. Hers are poems to read straight through, a paradoxical bacchanal of the senses for ethicists. This tender poet draws from the most unpromising materials poems of middle mid-western America as fiercely resistant to its hatreds as they are fiercely enraptured of its bodies."
—Shirley Geok-lin Lim, author of *What the Fortune Teller Didn't Say, Among the White Moon Faces*

"In *Throat* Mary Ann Wehler chronicles the history of the body and the education of the soul. 'There must be an easier way,' she says in a poem about a daughter's brain surgery. But in fact there isn't, and Wehler knows it. There is, instead, a continual broadening of affections in these poems that count the cost of love, and then love all the more. Wehler moves from grief to compassion, from longing to acceptance, with a lot of impressive honesty along the way. In a triumph of human spirit she converts the legacy of her father's racism and disappointment into a fierce commitment to justice and a determined embrace of life—evidenced by her attentiveness to beauty and anguish both, her frank celebration of pleasure, and her deep care for those at the fragile beginnings and ends of life."
—Betsy Sholl, author of *The Red Line*

THROAT

POEMS

Mary Ann Wehler

Midwest Writers Series
Bottom Dog Press
Huron, Ohio

Acknowledgments on page 103

Cover Art by Cathy Heno-Suffel
She is known for her unique collage paintings.

Dedication

Thanks to Jim Wehler, my true love, and first editor, my children who tolerate my obsession with writing and at the same time admire the fact that a grandmother wants to write, my advisors in the MFA program at Vermont: Rick Jackson, Betsy Scholl, Natasha Sajë, & David Wohjahn, and many teachers I have had over the years, the Writer's Voice poetry workshop group, M.L. Liebler, Director of the Writer's Voice, the students in my workshops who constantly amaze me, all the editors who have recognized the worth in my writing, especially Larry Smith of Bottom Dog Press who published my first poem and is the publisher of this volume, my second book of poetry.

Bottom Dog Press
PO Box 425
Huron, Ohio 44839
Lsmithdog@aol.com

Contents

I. Choke

II. Swallow

III. Throat

IV. Passage

I. Choke

…writing the poem helped her to survive,
helped him to live.
                                    -Gregory Orr

There's a Condo in Florida

It's not just that she's old or that her caregivers fight
like biddy hens or that her toe is infected
and she cries all night, cries every night to these women
who watch her for ten dollars an hour, so that they
ice her aching toe, slip into the bed
next to hers. It's not because five
or six times a year for the last ten years, I've
crawled back in my dead father's bed. Last week,
I sent a pressed pansy and a new maple leaf.
She sobbed, *All I want in life is to sit in your new
backyard.* She'd been arguing with the caregiver
about rice pudding, because this pudding doesn't taste
like hers. *Do you remember my recipe?* The one she made
for everyone in the condo when they were dying,
first the husbands, later the wives.
She'd send me to the store for Half & Half,
rice so good for digestion, the taste buds change
with radiation. She'd pick two gardenias, take one
with rice pudding to Mabel dying in # 4,
come back with a flower for herself, always a bloom
in season on the table filling the room with scent.
It's not just glaucoma, cataracts, or broken blood vessels,
ten crushed vertebra, osteoporosis, the oxygen tubes
from her nose and ears like an astronaut traveling
outer space. She keeps losing her hearing aids
and her daughter, me, living up in Michigan. It's not just
that I pray she'll die soon; no, we'll sit at the table,
I'll finger the plastic placemat, notice the dirt on the carpet,
slide nursing home brochures over, tears on my cheeks.
It is the tears with the call every day, the pull of guilt
like magnets on her icebox when she tells me
I should be there and last night she was sure
was her last. I hold the phone, imagine I smooth hair
off her forehead, wipe her brow, enfold her hand,
feed her the way we fed my father on his last day.

Dance Naked

Your skin, cheeks, and eyes,
your fingers, testicles, and penis,
your voice.
Don't let
last night
be the final time
you enter me.
The phone doesn't ring; the doctor should
have called with test results tonight.
I sit silent and wait, pretend
to read.

My father lost his erections
to cancer. They bought twin beds.
I visited mom,
lay on my dead father's bed,
thought, *What did you do?*
How did you stand it?
I don't want to give
up the thrill of your hands
on my body.
So, we wait,
watch the Oscars,
where the screen fills with breasts in skimpy dresses.
Demi Moore announces to the women of the world,
Dance naked for yourself.

Nightmare

The camera caught her hands clutched under
her chin, eyes squeezed shut. She was wrapped in a tarp.
They were pulling her over rocks, jolting
down the mountain. Photos from Kosovo,
but I keep seeing my mother,
cowering on the ground, misery in
her eyes, separated from her children.
A man from the news walked through my bedroom
pushing a wheelbarrow, her arms and legs straddling
the sides, I was looking in my mother's eyes.
A refugee leads a reporter up
a snowcapped mountain. In a tent, old women,
all my mother, gawk, hugging their legs,
some squatting, some lying down, cratered eyes of fear.

Visiting Hour

If this were played upon a stage now, I could
condemn it as an improbable fiction.
                    -William Shakespeare

I ring the locked ward buzzer, think, *How did you hang*
yourself, with all these precautions? Oh Anne, Oh Anne.
The guard checks me through a window, points over
to the "activity room." Past the pool table, the bandaged
cue sticks, the ping-pong table, and coffee machine,
you sit in a long-sleeved sweat shirt, hiding scars
you tore in your arms. Rope burns circle your neck.
A man sits and weeps. An anorexic fills her coffee cup,
clutches a smashed cigarette pack. Her hands shake,
she asks people for the time, wanders in and out.
A teenage boy, four-inch vertical scars across arteries
on his neck, comes in, cases the area, leaves. I want
to hold you, rock you, I remind myself not to cry.
You can't leave this room, can't even sit on the patio.
You hurt yourself. A staffer shadows you, sits, looks
at a magazine, glances at us over the top, takes notes
on a clipboard, listens to our small talk. Stiff from
Thorazine, a woman in a housecoat walks in robot-like.
Smoking's allowed for ten minutes, at ten minutes to
the hour. It's 7:48. Every patient holds a cigarette.
A woman, seventy, sits across from us. *Two cigarettes*
an hour, fourteen hours a day, three days, this is not
enough! She is trying to decide if forty cigarettes will
last 'til her son's next visit. You hung from your clothes
in this ward unsupervised for two minutes. I am terrified.
You're not getting better, no place in Michigan can help.
A Denver clinic will take you at $20,000 a week. I have
the plane tickets. What else can I do? The man weeps,
the anorexic with stringy hair returns for coffee; you wear
a sweatshirt to cover your scars. The temperature is 95.
Visiting hour over; I kiss you good-by, hug you and hug
you. I choke and say, *Remember, I love you, Anne.*
You reply, *I'm fighting to stay alive.*

I Can Hardly Laugh From Crying

The minute I get in their house,
my two grandchildren grab my hands,
pull me up the stairs. *Come see my bedroom.*
Dean puts his hands on his hips,
tilts his head with a look of *Well,*
what do you think? I've seen the dump trucks,
fire trucks, tow trucks on walls and sheets
many times. He's saying, *This is my space.*
Leah shouts, *My room, my room!* They both
tear down the hall and climb into her crib.
Cover me, cover me. Once more I cover them.
Kiss me, kiss me. I kiss them. *Say it, say it!*
I say, *Don't let the bed bugs bite.* Then,
Close the door! I close the door, they jump up
screaming. I open the door, they flop back down.
Cover me, cover me! Kiss me, kiss me!.

King of My World

I cupped his tufted hair, slid him in his bath,
wrapped him perfect in a towel, talked to eyes
that everywhere followed me. I held his whole body
on my legs, new head nestled on my knees, scooped
applesauce or squash to his snapdragon mouth.

He rode the Sear's red trike down the block,
pumping legs blurred by spokes. His lips were
the motor for a jeep or cement truck. David tore
up the drive, sun sparkled sweaty head, bounded
in for a drink and back to his work riding tricycles.

Years later, how can I tell it? He woke
me after midnight, afraid of those voices.
And – there was the knife. The first emergency
room said it was *just one psychotic episode*.

Crazy laugh, spooky eyes, my first-born, I must
learn to love his slow, bow-legged walk,
the coffee cup seated on his belly, the twitching
knee, the half grin when he doesn't get it.

Headquarters

For my Brother, Bill

*Hello, calling Headquarters! This is Bill — Do you hear
me? Come in! Come in!* At my parents' farm, brother
Bill strung his walkie-talkie from a blanket tent to the house,
a call to mother, *Do you hear me?* He played cars under

the dining room table, used the rungs for roads. The only
time I knew he existed was when I tripped over his toy
jeep in my heels. On my way to a dance or party, I'd
scream, *Mom, if I break my neck, you'll be sorry!*

Last night, I talked to Mom; she's 95. Every day's call
starts with, *How was your day, Mom?* Days spent in bed,
she says, *Not so good.* Thank god, Bill had been there,
sixty now himself. She starts to cry, tells me the washing

machine's broken. *I told him to cut off my nightgown. He
wouldn't.* She doesn't want to say she lost control of her
bowels. *He had to scrub the carpet. Mary Ann, he never
saw me naked before. He went to the Laundromat. I'm*

wearing a diaper. What a mess! Her voice is shaky,
weak. I call the airline, get a reservation for as soon
as possible. *Mom! Mom! Do you hear me?
Do you hear me? I need to get to headquarters.*

She Keeps Up With The Times Reading Harlequins

Mother's life rolls over me like Atlantic storms.
Her hearing aids tumble on the bedclothes;
washed-up seashells, the cartilage in her ears
soft clams. She surfs TV, swims about in Oprah,
calls through the spray, *Is that too loud?*
My head roars. Oprah talks about Aids.
I holler to Mom that my friend will die
from Aids. At commercial her hospital bed
crests above me. *It's not their fault,*
they were born that way, right?
Right! I stick my toe carefully in that sea.
Well, she says, *I've always wondered*
what they did. I'm drowning.
Grit of avoidence on my tongue,
I paddle away. *Beats me,*
I'm going to wash the dishes.

The Rapture of Fear

Fingers and hands, mouth
and tongue all over each other,
bedroom doorwall open
to our lakeside view.
Bodies touching, light
as a dragonfly feathering a petal;
fiercer then a gale over the lake,
and what if this was the last,
so miserly, I grasp and say, *Again,*
again, and tomorrow again.
Sweeping to rapture on the wings
of fear rather than love or lust,
the soul ready before the body.
Mother close to death, your surgery,
I lay in bed, exhausted, comforted,
watch the moon move over the sky.

Match Book Love/ Barlum Hotel Honeymoon

My mother, like a lost rag doll, slumps in her wheelchair,
surrounded by suitcases packed with teddy-bears
and dresses. She fought off life in a nursing home ten
years, regularly said, *Not while I'm in my right mind.*

Waiting for the ride to the airport, looking through
her wallet, making sure the Medicare, Blue Cross,
and Social Security cards were there, checking my purse
for her expired passport, photo ID, all for the last plane ride

of Edna's life. From her wheelchair she reached
for her wallet, I held back, *I'll keep it for you, Mom.*
Edna blankly stared at this unrecognizable person,
said, Just for a minute. Reaching in the wallet, she

lifted a leather flap, removed a two inch corner
of envelope. Slipping a matchbook from the wizened
paper she opened it and squinted at some writing.
One moment of lucidity and challenge, *I bet you don't*

have anything like this. It was from the Barlum Hotel,
Detroit, Michigan, eight hundred outside rooms
with combination bath and shower.
Rates: one person $2.50, two persons $4.00.

The inside cover read, *The happiest day in my life.*
Room 1110 with my own dear wife. 11-19-32.
For a blink she recognized her daughter, *I know*
All those things you wrote, but he loved me.

I slipped the match book back in its brittle edge, into
her wallet, zipped it safe in my purse. *Mom, that's so*
sweet, saved 67 years, I never knew you had it. She
flinched and glared, *I'm not your mother, you're mean*

to me, I want my old help back. Our ride to the airport
knocked at the door. Pushing her wheelchair to the car,

I remember pictures in an old photo album. Rakish tilt
of a fedora hat on my father's head, arm leaning on the roof

of a Model T Ford. Mother wrapped in a sealskin collared
black coat. Married by a Justice of the Peace, they spent one
night at the Barlum Hotel. Rates: one person $2.50,
two persons $4.00, November 19, 1932, *He loved me.*

Waiting for the Taxi to the Airport on the Way
to the Nursing Home in Michigan

Kept me up all night, now I'm dumped in a wheelchair
by the front door surrounded by suitcases
and boxes. Doesn't she know I need the bathroom?
I wonder where all these boxes are going? That
luggage looks like mine. Mean helper, I'll fire her
tomorrow. Look, she's going through my purse
now. *Give me my purse!* Who does she think she is?
My daughter? Too old. *Yeah, well, show me your kids!*
I got her there. Look on my desk, my grandchildrens'
pictures are there. Well, they used to be. What does
she mean, "packed in boxes." People keep moving my
stuff. *Give me my wallet!* Who's she think she's kidding,
I won't let her steal my money. You can't trust the help
these days. Look at that, money's all gone. Well I'll
show her something I bet she never saw. *Here, look
at this, I know that stuff you wrote, but he loved me.*
If I had my glasses I could read it myself,
a matchbook from my honeymoon at the Barlum Hotel,
$4.00 a night in 1932.
Read about the happiest day of his life. Yes,
in room 1110 with me, who'd she think? Now
she's crying. Look at that–she put my wallet in
her purse. She says we're going to fly to Michigan.
She's full of B.S. I haven't lived in Michigan
for thirty years. *Hey you, take me to the bathroom,
don't hurt my arms when you lift me on the toilet.*
Tell you one thing, nobody's putting me in
a nursing home, not while I'm in my right mind.

She Can't Hear Me

She's been in the nursing home six days. Patients can't stay in their rooms unsupervised so Mother's kept in a wheelchair in the day room most of the day; her unelevated legs swell to double their size. I know after breakfast she must get to the bathroom. The day before she dies, she tells me, *I'm being punished if I don't finish my breakfast. Take me to the bathroom, quick.* While I strain to help her in an unfamiliar room, she says, *They won't let me use the toilet. I'm forced to hold it.*

Each aide is responsible for twenty-two patients. I ask for her hearing aids; someone grudgingly retrieves them from the locked medicine cabinet. It's hard enough communicating with Mom when her hearing aids are in. When I bring them, she's relieved; she thought she'd lost them or they'd disappeared just like her hearing aid case and lipstick on the first day. They have patients, called walkers, Alzheimer's, that dress in the dark and walk the halls, no sense of night or day, so things disappear.

I brought her back from a home visit Sunday evening, the halls stacked with patients in wheelchairs. They grab at my arms, hang on my shirt, beg me to help them to bed. I push my mother to her room, lift her dress above her head; even on this last night, she is careful to see her dress ends up right side out. I choose a nightgown, her name, *Edna Madsen*, ironed on in tape. I slip it over her head, sore arm first, left arm last, and move the chair towards the bathroom. I open the door; the floor and the toilet are covered with shit.

Her roommate sitting in her wheelchair, her naked bottom half covered with a red sweater, pleads, *I've been waiting for hours, nobody came.* I return to the nurses' station, I'm crying, *My mother needs to use the toilet, it's covered with feces.* An aide comes, grumbles, *This shouldn't be my job*, while she's cleaning; when she leaves, I look in, I still see stains on the toilet, wet toilet paper in bits on the floor. Her roommate says, *I think I have the flu.* Mother doesn't need the flu. No one offers to help me with her. Finally, I'm able to help mom to the toilet. I lift her into bed, hold her hearing aids, to be locked in the cabinet for the night. I reach in her purse for her rosary; she shakes her head, zips the purse shut and clutches it, her eyes squeezed shut. I cover her, kiss her, and whisper, *I love you.* She can't hear me.

Black Silhouette Against the Sky

At dusk, the blue heron fishes under our park
spotlight. In the morning his prints fill
lake shallows like webbed Hadrosaur feet
in Texas stone. Minnows, offspring of his twilight
supper, sweep the prints away as they scour
the sand for food. Tonight, past their bedtime,

neighbor children squeal near the shore, jump
from inner tubes, splash each other. From my patio,
I see the heron fly now like a giant Pterodactyl,
land atop the tallest tree in my yard, wait for swimmers
to leave his fishing ground. His shadow merges
with ash leaves, black silhouette against the sky,

breezes blend his shape with the tree. I strain my eye
to separate feather from leaf, as intricate as sorting
life's tangles. While I'm lost in thought, the heron vanishes,
gives up his hunt for tonight. Tomorrow he'll reappear,
assert his claim on this tiny lake one mile from his rookery.

Present Time

Near the end,
fingers grasped my arm
with a shimmery tremor;

she said, *Don't do this to me,*
not sure who I was, saint or ogre,
her mind drifting in and out of present

time, on the plane flying
to a nursing home near my house.
She floated on the brink

so often. I don't pray, but often
thought, *Please take her.*
Once she confessed to Father Brice

she wished she were dead.
Never again will she ask why
I don't go to mass. If there's a heaven,

make it sandy shores for her to stroll.
For me, it's Mother setting the table,
cooking the roast, knitting mittens,

calling her daughter, letting her know
how the beach is today. I would
know by her voice I was forgiven.

Never Say Never

black women
        minimum wage
assigned twenty inmates
        clean and dress
                shift at seven

breakfast by nine
        roll them out
parked in observation
        glazed eyes
                pain hoots

hands flail
        bloody shins
hall roaming
        the home chosen
                mother's last days
head nurse
        only nurse
in an office
        door half closed
                clients can't
be trusted
        to pick up a fork
don't worry (shock in my eyes)
        your mother won't
                eat with them
(she did)
        visiting day Sunday
parked in observation
        Mother sits
                twists her purse straps

needs a bathroom
        hurry the wheelchair
weeps *punishing me*
        hear in my head, *promise me*
                never a nursing home.

Her Clothes Still Lay in the Laundry Room

Last Sunday, I brought her home for dinner,
her first trip from the nursing home.
The five-mile trip so wearing, she napped
for an hour. She died on Monday.

Today is Tuesday, I thought I could
wash her sheets, go through her things.
I thought my mind was on other subjects.
I lifted the knit bed jacket to my nose–
all that's left is her scent,
there in the family room, there
on the La-Z-Boy where she slept. I left

her clothes and treasures on the basement
floor. When she went in the nursing
home, I kept her wallet, her checkbook,
her jewelry, her money. Today,
her purse felt hollow. Three zippers:
in one pocket, a piece of paper
with my phone number; in another,
her sunglasses, also wadded Kleenex
and menus for the five days
she spent in the home.

*They're punishing me, this isn't
a very nice lodge*, never sure where
I had brought her. And later *I can't
believe you'd do this to me.* Her feet
and legs swollen like balloons.

In Florida, she lay in bed like a queen,
feet tipped up to help the circulation.
I can see her spreading bills on the bedspread,
counting her money over and over, squinting
at the checkbook, trying to balance it.

Little Red

why does grandmother live in a shack on the far
edge of the woods

        should mother have sent little red out walking alone

           what was in the basket – pills,
           soup cookies Prozac

then there was the wolf – think nursing home –
who threw out the pills and devoured the money

           little red without a grandmother
mother filled with nightmares

           the woodcutter – read medicare –
           opens the wolf and raises the old lady out

by then her brain is addled
she can't recognize her daughter
or little red

           cowering in her rocking – wheel – chair
             wailing   HELP ME HELP ME

        until her lungs fill up with fluid

I'm the mother

           I trusted the wolf when he said
           grandmother doesn't need oxygen

wolf   woodcutter   little red   mother

the more I write this story

the more villains appear

Throat

Thrown over the bridge, no one heard them mew,
noose round a burlap bag filled with kittens, flung
from a stranger's car window to the stream on my father's
farm, raised a stench that kept us kids out of the creek
all summer. Some people gag on food, others choke

on words, Marcia kicked the chair from under herself,
hanged by her husband's tie. In nightmares, I see
her grab at her throat, shut off by words
never said to her lover, like a cloth sack, roiling
in her gut, a bad marriage and no exit, collared

in depression. What does that have to do with me
holding my brothers' hands as we stood together,
counted to three, leaped into the gravel pit?
My brother says our parents were crazy letting us
swim there. But the stream reeked of kittens. A hot

summer day before the headlines: *Landslide Buries
Kids in Gravel Pit.* Hand over hand, feet grip
like a circus act, the three of us tightrope the rusted
metal girders that carried the gravel shovel to the pit's
center, drop into the icy water, our goal to touch

the bottom with our toes, eyes squeezed shut, opening
in the green hazy deep to see where daylight was,
whether we were going up or down, pushing off
the mucky bottom. Marcia knew how to swim, may
have opened her eyes, struggling against the black.

II. Swallow

*...reading for what it says about their lives or what it doesn't say.
And they loved certain writings because of truths, understandings,
affirmations, that they found in them...*
                                                    -Tillie Olsen

Looking For Reasons

How many dogs and cats and parakeets are buried in back yards, the bird wrapped in a father's thinnest hankie, the dog or cat in an old shirt or a well-worn dish towel? My father put peanuts out to tempt squirrels. Once, he bribed one all the way into the living room, across the carpet and up on to the couch. I sat with feet tucked under resting on the fake leather brought home from G.M. I watched him reupholster in the middle of the living room, saw him pound his finger. He yelled at mother to get me out before I got hurt, I was making him nervous. My feet stayed gathered up on the chair,safe from wild things. Amazing, to think mother allowed such a mess in her clean living room.

A jay at the bird feeder invades my train of thought with his call. Every time I raise my head to think, I look out the window and see two scenes. The one happening right now, a bluejay scattering seeds, the other is Basho crossing mountains in summer snow. Sometimes I forget what zone I'm in. It seemed like a good idea to bring some of Mother's ashes back, sprinkle them in my flower garden; she loved flowers. That jay is at the feeder again, he warns chickadees and finches, caws them away. See that damn squirrel still digging up my yard. Basho carries everything he owns on his back; brushes, robe, small gifts it's bad luck to leave behind. My son, David walks away with nothing on his back, sells everything he owns to a roommate and takes off with just as many clothes as he can cram into his car. Laundromats are low priority; I save old towels.

Who washed Basho's other robe? The finch bathes in my lake, brave tiny bird, it flits in for a seed, in spite of the red tailed rat.When Basho writes of the long grass, Dean Young doesn't want to know it has to do with death. But what else is there to learn, what do feathers on the junco's back have to do with the jay? David calls from California—*I don't want you to worry about me*—and doesn't have to say his medicine has stopped working. Snow's predicted, the birds have left the feeder. I look for a reason, in the bare ash a red-tailed hawk is tearing at prey held in his claw.He may need towels soon. My mother used to pray for him. Half believing in an afterlife, I ask her to watch over my son.

Paper White Narcissus: *Narcissus tazetta*

Paper Whites, pebble set in shallow dish,
roots more dense each morning.

> *The farther traveled*
> *the deeper the search.*

The force of wild-hair root tendrils
lift Narcissus from their anchor.

> *A growth that lifts one out*
> *of circumstance, meddlesome.*

Crisp brown onion skin splits
to ivory center nurtures stem and bloom.

> *Words are my water*
> *reaching for reason.*

Tall green stems, multiplicity of bloom,
miniature, bareheaded, lean to light.

> *Thought sequesters.*
> *Knowledge shrieks.*

One nub late in stem and root, pluck
it out, place in a glass, it stands erect.

> *Revising, everything*
> *becomes a poem.*

Rooting. The deeper the foundation
the more constraining the container.

> *Oh – listen! The wind blows.*
> *The chimes sing. Paper-White.*

I Count Them Over, Every One Apart, My Rosary, My Rosary

-Robert Cameron Rogers

His father, my mother, clung to their faith, lifted eyes
to the alter, stumbled over mysteries of the rosary.
The closer they got to death, the more rote prayer
became. Both buried with beads, his father's tangled
through fingers, I see them slipping in the quicksand
of space, drowning in age, drifting into nothingness.
In the end, only their meal schedule kept them in touch
with life. Looking over this swamp called Purgatory,
with its gnarled hands lifted to the sky, struggling
in the slurp of sucking ground swell, most of the heads
have slipped under; occasionally, a pair of lips whisper,
Glory be to God. We buried them within a month
of one another. Mother in little packages, a box of bone
dust placed in her coffin next to her pink dress, ring
settings and a rose-colored rosary snapped up in its
case. Gaunt after two years in a nursing home, his only
suit cut by the embalmer to fit a shrunken frame. No
sign that their faith didn't let them down, Hell repeats
itself day after day. Last week, I lost the small box of ashes
meant to spread in my garden. They were on a shelf
in my writing room, waiting for me to get far enough
from grief that I might let the ash blow about my garden.
The only color left, a few cosmos tossing in the October wind.

Half a Century Later, A Sense of Being Held

Nothing to do, I sit on the top step of the back
porch painted surplus gray, feel the crack
between the two planks, pick the flaking paint.
My mother washes my hair, sends me to sit
in the sun, to brush it dry. Now, I'm on the second
step, she catches my body between her knees
and thighs. Mother's starched apron edges poke
my bare back where skin shines from my halter.

Two red rubberbands circle her wrist, she
braids my hair, pulls the comb, *hold still*,
through the bobbi pins in her mouth, squeezes
her knees when I wiggle. Reaching the end,
she takes the red, winds it round, tucks
the hair ends up, ties plaid ribbon over
rubber. I love the whiskery poke of hair
on my finger tips. I feel her legs,
right now, clasp me, keep me tight.

If Turtles Could Fly

The snapping turtle lived on the back porch in an aluminum washtub. My brother Jack fed him lettuce and carrots, hamburger and dog food. Paving-block shell, scratchy toenails, nose like a spear; his internal compass never missed the direction of water when we let him out to exercise. Jack explored the Detroit River, the woods, and ravines. I walked to dance school, window shopped on Jefferson Avenue. If I sat on the top wooden step, held a lettuce leaf above the turtle's nose, it clipped off bites with its razor teeth. I held the lettuce carefully, kept my distance. By his deathbed, the week my father would die, I called Jack; he said, *Keep me posted; let me know when to come. I'm no good with good-byes.* He flew down in time for the funeral. We stood outside the condo and caught twenty-one chameleons. Chain-smoking cigarettes, he trained his hunter eyes on the bushes. I held the jar, opened the lid when he caught a lizard. What do people have in common? With us it was plants and animals. We didn't talk pain or sadness, failure or fear. We didn't do that.

Baby hawks, on the porch one summer, were fed chopped meat. I don't know where he got them. That's how I felt when my brother finally came down to Florida, our father already dead. Jack got drunk; he did that then. *You may be older, but I'm the head of the family now.* He said a lot of mean things. Mother said they didn't mean it, Jack and my Dad, when they used cruel words. Sober now, he tells me he loves me. He doesn't have hawks or turtles; he collects plants. He's lost his children and his wives and he's sorry and alone, except for the three hundred plants in his apartment. I remember a dog; I'm not crazy about dogs. It leaped at the front screen door, I was nine, ready to pounce on me as soon as I opened the door. His front paws on my shoulders. he bit at my clothes, scratched my skin. After awhile, he disappeared. I don't miss him.

When Jack was a teenager, he owned a canoe with his buddy. He'd laugh when he told how the canoe caught in the wake of a freighter, the ship threw out waves that capsized their canoe in the Detroit River. Jack and Fred hung on the sides, almost drowned. That's life–you see someone you care about come up for the third time, all you can do is hang onto the side and hope you stay alive.

Smooth Sidewalks

The best sidewalk for skates, half-way down the block,
brand new cement in front of two houses, I could turn,
skate backwards, stop on my toes. I was Sonja Henie.

The Kummer boys captured me in the middle of a dream
turn, my hands posed above my head. They dragged
me into their garage. *You guys are gonna be in trouble!*

But they tied me to a chair near the smudged window,
the spider webs. I smelled the old newspapers piled
in the corner, the case of brown beer bottles,

its lid flapped open to take the next empty. Donald
poked my stomach with a stick. *You're the enemy.*
I thought of the possibility of rat nests. I heard

the boys whisper, giggle in the corner. Their mother
called them from the porch. *Supper time.* Untying
me they warned, *You'll be sorry if you tell, we'll get you.*

The cool feel of the skate key that hung from my neck;
I sucked the end of it, stuck the tip of my tongue
in the square hole, pressed the shape on the skin of my arm.

Facing the Flame

As Mother shovels coal, I lift hands against the flame
try to get closer but the heat burns my eyes and arms.

I back off, mesmerized by her face lit red and gold.
She shakes the stoker, pokes and rattles cinders,

clinkers falling through the grate. What nerve to lift
the handle, slam the iron door on the fire imprisoned

behind the intricate metal work. Octopus arms
send heat upstairs, where I sit on the radiator,

warm my body cold mornings, smell coal smoke.
You're old enough to light the tank. The holes

where the gas escapes lie like the inner side
of a tentacle, wait to grab and suck life from me.

When she points to them, I turn the spigot, strike
and throw the match, heart flaming in my chest.

1943

We lived on the border. I never knew why I walked over a mile to Guyton Elementary when Keating was so close. I never questioned why I was allowed to ride my bike on Grosse Pointe streets, never towards Conner Avenue and the old Hudson plant. One black family, the father a doctor, lived in a big house on Marlborough Boulevard. The only street I knew paved with bricks. Riding my bike, I'd pretend I was on the Road to Oz. Even the porch was brick, not wood like ours. Two wooden rocking chairs with ruffled cushions, a rug spread beneath; no one ever sat there. The doctor's son was the only black child at Guyton. Most folks were renters.

When my father started on the day shift, eating supper with us, words like *nigger, polack,kike, and spick* were served with the meal. He mouthed J. Edgar Hoover's FBI alleging Mrs. Roosevelt had Negro blood.If I snuck a ride in the wrong direction most faces on the porch were brown or black. 1943, year of the Belle Isle riot, four miles from my house, WW II, I never got that far. No one on my street had a car. The fathers took buses or streetcars to the auto plants,built tanks or airplanes. Mothers walked to the grocery store daily, held ration stamps in their handbags. *The Detroit News* said, "Eleanor Roosevelt urges Detroit to allow Blacks in the Sojourner Truth Housing Project." Next in pecking order, the Polish community, didn't know Sojourner was an African Heroine, but objected. 200 Negro families were moved into the project; the riots began. Weren't there whispers, talk on my block? Was it kept from me?

June, 1943, our street, Piper, the border, between rich and blue collar, a street of flats. No rockers on the porches; people sat on the steps. Twenty-five years later, driving from the airport to their Florida condo, Father baited me. *Niggers live on the other side of Federal Highway,* watching for my reaction in the rearview mirror, he couldn't wait to start a fight. That night Flip Wilson clowned on "The Ed Sullivan Show," *Makes you believe in evolution.* Having a daughter who knew he'd been scared all his life stuck in his craw. He's buried in a vault in Boca, safe from his hates.

Talons

I never spoke of the heat in my vagina,
the fire as I healed from child birth. Like

a climax, contractions in the tumescent womb
coursed as the newborn nursed, my mother ear

hearing the least babe's whimper, milk hastening
through nipples, staining shirts. *Change your clothes!*

my first husband fumed, *I can't
help if you insist on doing this.*

Each night, him hungry for sex,
baby's small bleat spilled blue opalescense.

Leaping from our bed, he'd drop the squalling child
still wrapped like a papoose, storm out

to full blast TV waking the boy.
My body turned numb, sour smell of spittle

on my chest. Bone tired, life's dirty trick,
no strength for even a moment to twine

bodies, legs. Dr. Halakas slammed, *What
did you expect?* My body's urgency wanes.

Chick in the nest, I swallowed the urge
to unsheath my claws – stronger every day.

Centering

Pull tacks from the back of a chair,
push the tool deep
in the fabric. Meantime, my daughter

Anne needs brain surgery. Working
in the center
of the garage, I drop nails in a pail

one at a time. Let the mail bring
news of a cure.
Like opening an envelope,

I pull fabric from the chair back,
reveal another
layer. The surgeon will remove

the first disc in her spine, gently
set her skull down.
You must take time, find the center.

Someone took a shortcut upholstering
this chair. I rub
walnut arms, smooth as bone, caress

fine curve, spine of chair. Who sat
before me? Head of table,
this old chair. Push and dig, over years.

A mother may have nursed her child
as I suckled Anne.
At six, she sat between my legs,

I brushed her long hair. This chair's been
finished two ways.
I'll keep in mind the last, undo

the original cloth, remember
the lace dress bought
in Le Puy before she was imagined.

The neuro-surgeon knows his trade.
I yearn to hold and rock.
My breasts that nursed numb with worry.

What Shall I Say Because Talk I Must...

-W. C. Williams

My love so strong, I refuse to hold
her head, or the secret, or the bowl.
She will either get better or die,
flesh on bone scantily gaunt.
A Kosovo orphan could feed for a week
on food flushed down her toilet.

Caught between the pages of the latest
fashion 'zine or TV, this *Spirit Child*
subsists on chicken breast, lettuce & water,
clips off to work in high-heeled shoes.
In high-cut skirts, power suits, she succeeds
in America's corporate world. Men ogle
those scrawny legs, flat chest, sunken cheeks,
sallow skin. Mesmerized by her painted eyes,
they listen as she spouts stock options, six
figures, 401k's, retirement packages.
Pamela, who are you kidding?

David, My Perfect Child

His belly hangs over his pants
like the frosting that dripped on his 44th
birthday cake. His breath is the rasping
of a saw cutting down a neighbor's

tree. He coughs and sputters
more than the teapot on the stove,
face bloated from medication,
eyes slits in flesh. He walks

through my house like a stiff-legged Buddha.
His coffee cup drips conspicuously
down the stairs, across the rug to a chair.
Awake through the night,

I feel the vibration of his feet
as he walks out the doorwall, working
on his second pack of Camels.
I'm going out to feed the monkey.

As they moved away, the other children
took their baby albums; I've kept his.
Together, we choose pictures for a woman
making a TV special about mental patients

attending junior college, learning to be
support staff for the San Mateo health
system. David's part of a success story,
so we pick the most appealing; then he says,

*I better take this one. You can see
I'm in trouble. Look at my eyes.*
My perfect child, today he's on his way
home to California where he lives alone.

Twisted Sheets

I remember hair hanging down
to her waist. As she gathered the sheet
to feed through the wringer, her hair wound
round her throat, tangled up in the fabric
as it spun through the rollers. She must
have screamed. Two toddlers napped
in cribs, no one heard, no one came.
My school principal called me out in the hall.
While he whispered, I watched my kids
do math. Mist filled the room
where Jenny sat. She was absent a week.
When she came back, her hair had been cut,
Dutch-boy short. She returned with a smile
as if no one had told her how her mother died.
 After that at recess, Jenny stayed
by my side, held my hand tight. Her back yard
faced the playground, once, her father
was out hanging clothes on the line.
We watched him shake the twisted sheets,
struggle to keep them off the ground,
slowly pin them on the line. Running
her fingers through her own cropped tresses,
she told me, *My mother had long hair.*

Learning

Mary Ann McGee did not learn to read
in my first grade.
Each day, before she hung up her coat,

she threw her arms round my middle
and said, *I love you.*
What she meant was, *I feel safe now.*

Mary Ann McGee's mother had cancer
before she had Mary Ann.
She lived for five years after her birth.

Mary Ann would whisper, *Take me home
with you, tonight.*
One arm lost in a war, her father spent

most days and evenings at Joe's Bar
drinking beer
and shots. Mary Ann did homework

with the waitress in a dark corner,
but she didn't
learn to read. Once after school,

her father stopped by to fill me in.
Mary Ann knew how
to wash clothes, make beds better

than him, make her breakfast and lunch,
help with the shopping.
When her mother was in bed dying,

Mary Ann McGee, five years old,
was the caretaker.
I told him how I had tried and tried

to teach Mary Ann to read. Patting me
with his one hand,
he said, *She can do more than me,*

I'm right-handed, and I don't have one.
She's smart, my girl,
 you watch, she's busy this year,

don't worry,
Mary Ann McGee,
she'll learn to read.

Father's Last Night

Your body is wasted by radiation.
Just a few drops of water
pass your lips.
I lift the infant spoon to your mouth.
Your throat works to swallow,
like a newborn learning to sip,
water running down your chin.
Clouds cover your eyes.
Your lids flicker
with the effort to see.
Each hour, your body is turned,
as on a parched spit
of starved bones,
lest bedsores invade your
racked, tired frame.
You lay naked beneath
the thinnest white sheet,
while we attend you.
You mewl in pain as fever
burns your skin.
Your wife dabs oil on your
shriveled penis. I recall
anointing my infants
with the same loving care
my mother extends
this last night of your life.

At Ten, I Was a Boy, Sometimes

Boys don't have to bathe, worry
about their hair, put on makeup,
no one ever tells them to be careful
riding their bike, zipping, zooming,
flying 'round the block, wheels spinning
fast as possible. Legs spread wide,
hands wider, the breeze stands hair
on end, whistles in your ears, dries
your eyes, while you fly nohanded
and if the cement is rough enough
open your mouth and breathe out loud,
the buzz tickles the roof of your mouth,
down your throat. After the bike ride
charge up the back stairs, stomp so hard
the wood trembles through your legs,
feel the motion in your crotch. Lie
in the grass blowing spit bubbles,
let them run down your chin, over
your neck. Later, stretch on the front porch
your ear on the wood, the sound
of the player piano in the flat upstairs
plinking in your ears sounds louder,
brilliant. Take a pin from mother's
pin cushion to the alley, sit behind
the garage, pick initials in the top
of your hand, squeeze each pin prick
until the blood breaks your skin, scabs.
Write your name, the name you want
to be called, use chalk and scrawl it
across the front sidewalk, *Call me John,*
Big John. My name is Big John. Take
a stick, walk the length of the alley,
knock every flower poking through
a fence off its stem. Whack them, rip
them, decimate them, destroy them,
look back in glory at petals strung
out the block length; you're a famous
Spanish bull fighter or Superman

flying over New York. Then shut
the door to your room and shred
every Kotex in the box, pull them
apart, fling them in a plain brown
bag, throw them in the trash because
you'll never use those things.

Pulse

Behind the pills in Mother's kitchen, a chameleon
stares at me. Two inches nose to tail, he scoots
behind the bottles with nitro, blood and heart pills.
I slide the drugs away from the wall, try to catch
him in a tissue. He darts behind the breadboard,
freezes next to breakfast crumbs. His pulse throbs
through the skin on his back. I pounce again;
he leaps off the counter, lands on the lid of a waste
basket. Mother calls for help with her oxygen. He slips
down to hide on the floor. That night, the beat in my ear,
my own pulse, matches the motor whirr
pumping mother's air. I fall asleep to dream
green chameleons climb palm trees curled
like phone cords toward the sky.
Heartbeats, motor groan, labored breath.

Her Pocketbook

There's an edge of sorrow on my blue sky.
Papers rifled by September breeze.
Near the shore, a heron watches, statue-like, for fish.
Squirrels dash about with green-husked walnuts.
Next week, I'll be sixty-six, old enough for wisdom.
On a Monday, two weeks ago, my mother died.
The nursing home called in the middle of the night.
The nursing home called in the middle of the night
on a Monday, two weeks ago. My mother died.
Next week, I'll be sixty-six. Old enough for wisdom?
Squirrels dash about with green-husked walnuts
near the shore. A heron watches, statue-like, for fish.
Papers. Rifled by September breeze,
there's an edge of sorrow on my blue sky.

III. Throat

Whatever happened, I said yes, and discovered that every time I said it I could see further, more completely.
-Alicia Ostriker

Mason City Ladies' Sewing Circle

Fiddle fern hangs near corner porch column, scent
of Honeysuckle suspends in air, swing sways
at porch end, lemonade pitcher, glasses,
sliced lemons, plated ice-box cookies set on
wicker serving table, calico cat naps
on railing crook, rainbow glints off cut glass framed
in Grandmother Susan's mahogany front door,
baskets of mending sit near rattan rockers,
flashing in and out of fabric, needles spark
like the bullfighter's sword, the Spanish dancer's
stiletto heels. The sewing club murmurs,
Ronnie's croup, Ellie's scars from pox, how
their gardens grow, soon pokeberry-jelly time.
Some quiet complaint about how hard husbands'
work at not working, and they sew. Heels and toes
of socks woven in and out, knees of jeans, blue
chambray elbows, christening gown buttons, fine
stitches on collars of Sunday church-going dresses,
the flour sacks are last–

pick up the sacks and sew hoods. The hoods fathers,
husbands, and sons wear when they pound flaming
crosses in yards at night. They sew hoods for sowers
of corn fields in Iowa. With stopped-up throats
they sew hoods, murmur about the boy strung up
in the willow, country road outside Mason City.
For Don, the boy who sweeps the grocery store
after school each day, Susan sews a hood. The grocer
laughs with men who sit near the pot-bellied stove,
cold in May, laughs as they brag about a night they
dragged that nigger roped behind their truck, left him
by the river, served him right, opens the cash box,

hands the boy a dime. Grandmother Susan, father used
her name with a god-like reverence. He'd look at me
and say no one could match my mother, she was
a saint. Grandmother Susan saved her flour sacks,
sewed my father's hood, placed on his head, carefully

felt with fingers, so as not to hurt her first
born's eyes, marked with pins where to cut the sockets,
sewed the hood. Whose car did he ride in; who could
possibly catch him? His father, county sheriff
and game warden, threw his rifle along side length
of rope, fishing gear, and the hoods in the trunk. Late
summer nights, too hot to sleep, Grandmother
Susan sits with her daughter on the porch swing,
they count fireflies, admire her moon flowers.
A familiar car drives by, filled with men and boys
wearing hoods, what's that caught in her throat as she
turns her child's head, *Look, the moon is full tonight.*

The Soul Selects Her Own Society–Then–Shuts the Door

-Emily Dickinson

I come home late at night from college, walk
through the living room. He doesn't look up
from his paper, say hello. When it's time
for Prophet Jones on TV, he calls me
from my room, *Come here, look at this nigger
covered with gold.* Leaning close on his Early
American couch, part of a room full
of furniture bought cheap for this rented
lower-east-side flat, intent on the screen,
he yells, *That monkey owns ten Cadillacs,
I don't have a car; it doesn't make sense.*
He waggles his finger at the rings,
the weight of gold chains, *He looks like
a pansy up there on that throne.* Father's failed
get-rich schemes lie heavy in his acid gut.
*Look at me, the perfect example
of how not to end up.* When I defend
my black friends, he replies, *Sending you to
college was my biggest mistake. You've been
nothing but trouble since the day you were born.*

Until the Stitches Come Out

Green metal chair, Chicago porch, I try
to be five years old, watch the workman
across the street mix mortar from cement

bags and sand, a house of bricks, cement block,
stones. The surgeon opened my daughter's
skull, took a saw and cut a four-inch hole.

The cement mixer turns; a young black man
pours bucket after bucket of mortar
and water into its guts. The recipe

seems whim; he pours, runs and stops the machine,
stirs with a stick like cake batter. Laid in
a four inch patch, the staples run from her

nape to where the skull extends in back.
Wheelbarrow waits for its pour. After it's
full, the guy runs the barrow to scaffolds

at the side of the house, fills buckets to hoist
up to the second floor where brickers wait.
In a blue dumpster remnants of the old

house rest. My daughter stubs cigarettes on
the bottom step, throws her butts in the dumpster.
Looking like a roadway with hair on each side,

sixteen staples slide up the back of her
shaved head. Give the skull bone a chance to heal,
I think. Every ten or twenty minutes

out she comes for another smoke. Cement
in buckets pulled up on the rope, slathered
on cement block and brick. There must be

an easier way. A boy rides his bike,
stops to study lengths of wood leaning near
a garbage can. All those pills doctors gave

her, all those tests, neurologists, acupuncture,
pain-management clinics. A homeless man
in a purple shirt, earphones, baseball cap,

walks the alley. Three Mexican girls, four
to nine, stand under a tree in pink Target
sundresses; their brother takes a picture.

The endless drone of cement, Anne's been
sick a long time. Circles under her eyes,
she slept twenty-four hours at a time.

The mother comes out, hip-straddling a baby,
bends to buckle the infant. Her stretch pants
show lines of a thong, the story of starch

and five children. Adjusting bra straps under
her tank top so they only show in back
like the stitches the doctor will take out.

Mother's Ashes

Three days since she died and you can't touch or
see her dust, you haven't the courage. The small
sealed box in your suitcase, you bring to Michigan,
forget where the safe spot for ashes was
in your house, scramble about in your lingerie
drawer before a shower, wonder what it's doing there.

Winter cold, you move them to a shelf
in your writing room, stare at the box, hear
her voice the one time she was in your house.
What's all that white out there? Fogged eyes, blinded,
she couldn't distinguish lake or garden,
the only two things she wanted to see,

not the nursing home. Jim pours all the ash
in one nervous pile in front of the brightest
red poppy, red her favorite color.
He didn't know. Days when you're near the garden,
you stretch past the daisies, black-eyed susans,
cone flowers, ash still visible a month
later, the visceral feeling that she's
near by, like yoga or Zen, like sipping wine.
You even talk to her sometimes, a year now,
sorrow smoothed round like stone saved from the sea.

Jay

Can Cranes cogitate?
                    -Ruth Stone

A jay buries an acorn in the lawn outside
my window, lifts an oak leaf with his beak, conceals
his store. I am stunned. Most astonishing,
my use of the pronoun.

No one can grasp the sex of this jay, loud and irascible,
taken back by its shadow, I assumed a male.
What if this one's a female called away,
like women are called, from the wash, the dishes,
the writing, by a loud caw. What if *she*

were protecting her gain? Every lass ought
to have a cache. A second later,
I saw it, she yanked the leaf aside, plucked
the acorn from its hidey hole, took wing.

Stilled Time

The wind off the lake blows chairs
across the lawn as wind chimes
peal to the earth.

*

A pair of mallard ducks nose
round the front bushes. Our bed
is impossible to make today.

*

Changing clocks forward to Spring,
the bedroom alarm is neglected.
Time stilled for an hour.

*

My fingers ache with a fever
to dig in the soil and sparrows lift
straw from the flower bed.

...Life Understood Backwards; ...Lived Forward

-Sören Kierkegaard

last night I had to share him
  it seemed in the dream
    all women shared a man

curious I go back to bed
  try to return in sleep
    dream the why

walk in our garden
  each flower   every bud
    reminds me of sex

Poppy with deep purple
  center   Japanese Iris
    its labial folds

longing probes the center
  like a Swallowtail's
    proboscis sucks

each flower head delicious
  to view modest Coral Bells
    brazen Shastas cherry Cones

humming birds dip beaks
  in sweet liquor
    deep in Million Bells

yesterday I stood above him
  brushed my nose in
    his hair like silver anthers

the grandeur of flocks of purple
  pansies   electric touch
    his lips on my neck

Nests

At the breakfast table this morning, looking
up from my scrambled eggs, a pair
of mallards nosed about on the bricks outside
the door wall. So close, I could study their orange

webbed feet, see the lines of the brick coming through
between their toes. They've been fucking for weeks,
but now the female is on a serious hunt
for a nest. At my window, poking her beak

into every nook. I want to tell her to hole
up under the deck. I remember quail eggs
hatching at school, candling them so my students
could see the chick fetus that would hatch

in an incubator. Without parents, those chicks
knew how to eat and drink, huddle together
under light when they were cold. The father
duck's head and neck, iridescent green, beautiful,

he follows faithfully after his mate; he's had his fun.
Our own offspring grown, we're in a new home,
love last night, tangled like new lovers.

Breath

All summer long she slips into the lake,
three or four times a day, in one
of her many swim suits, paddles out
to the middle. Her husband, older,

maybe eighty, sits on the porch.
I hear him from the garden where I weed,
You're out too far, come in now.
Last week, he had a fine maple

chopped down, ground into chips.
When the water's too cold, she hauls
a bucket about the yard, picks up
leaves. His bad back doesn't want

her bending so much. I've only seen
him once this year, holding a stick,
hollering, *Did you see where the raccoons
went?* I wanted to say, *Looking*

*for a new home, you've chopped their house
down.* The raccoon home shaded
my patio of an evening. In the Spring,
back from Florida, she will scoot

around their yard picking up sticks,
tipping her toes in the lake, and, long
before Fourth of July, she'll be
in the middle, looking the other way.

He'll holler, *Too far!* She'll
continue to tread, tracking the heron,
watching the ducks, counting the geese
on the other end of the lake.

Nightwatch

Every night, my husband opens the bedroom
window. I listen as the geese
settle down on the lake. I hear a faraway honk,

like a dog barking. Tonight, I am sleepless.
I can't pick up
the sound of geese. I slip out of bed, walk

around in the dark of my new home, gaze out
over moonlit water,
through windows in every room. Our children

are grown, I wonder if they wander in the dark,
spread so far
across this continent, I don't know where to look.

I Was a Pool Shark at the Jefferson Avenue Y.M.C.A.

I

When the pre-war furnace was converted to gas, when Mother
stopped shoveling coal, she scrubbed the black dust from rafters, walls
and floor. Together, my parents painted the 5x8 ft. coal bin, turning it into a
tiny recreation room, my brothers' Christmas present, a folding

2 ½ x 4 ft. pool table was set up. I played pool in the scrubbed-out coal bin.
I'd rack those balls, move 'round the table, alone, or with Dad
when my brothers were out, I in their territory. Dad taught me how to keep
score, how to bounce one ball off another, get two in one shot.

My goal was to knock those balls, *Three in the side pocket*, s*even
in the corner.* Stand up, look tough, take a deep breath, basement bouquet
of mildew, spaghetti cooking, Oxydol swishing in the old Maytag wringer
washer, gas escaping from the old hot-water tank.

II

I was a pool shark at the Jefferson Avenue Y.M.C.A. Friday nights, women
could enter the inner sanctum of the Y., first floor only, the rest mysterious,
just as much a mortal sin as when I opened the door of the east-side
Lutheran church and placed my right foot inside. Who did I

aim my cue stick at as I played billiards and pool? At the Y., I could lean
my hip into mahogany, press my leg against a boy, show I knew how to
twist the tip of the cue into chalk, demonstrate how to hold
the stick under the ring finger of my left hand, run it along my index

finger, slide it back and forth, take aim, and pray that the seven ball fell into
the pocket. The vinyl spinning in the darkened meeting room,
a dance floor for Friday night only. I knew all the lyrics, hummed along,
wondered if my opponent would ask for a dance when the game

was over. If he said, *How about another game?,* I knew he couldn't dance.
If he suggested we move to the dance floor, I made a trip
to the ladies' room, met him by the music. If you're 14, and you have no
boobs, it's a good idea to check the Kleenex in your bra, make sure

it hasn't shifted to some strange place. I loved to dance, but sweat
formed on my upper lip as I anticipated a slow song, someone pulling

my body close. I was allowed to come home on the streetcar alone,
eleven o'clock curfew, nobody worried, except maybe me, walking

down that long block, Jefferson to Freud. In Detroit, we said *Frude*,
and it was a street name, extra dark, hundred-year-old maples, black
umbrellas over sidewalk and street. I counted the sidewalk cracks
between the streetlights till I got to Freud. Wonder what he'd have

thought of my damp pants. In heat—I wasn't even sure of what
I was after. Eight houses from the corner, 656 Piper, porch light
on, I took the steps two at a time, unlocked the door. *Yeah, it's me.*
Yeah, I had a good time. Yeah, I turned off the porch light.

Take Back

The Flowering Tree Ceremony comes from an American Indian custom. I'm told they dug a hole under a huge tree and called down their grievances. The tree I envision is an ancient Fig tree in the cemetery where my father is buried.

I will visit the flowering tree,
and leave the pain from father.
I will lie by the ancient Fig,
and send his fear and hatred
down the trunk into the roots,
deep in the bowels of the earth.
Let him pick up his fear,
let him take his hatred and anger,
let him know his own trouble,
let him know his own ignorance.
If he is sloshing in guilt,
why should I go along?

Let him be the bigot.
Let him be the small human.
Let him take his unforgiveness.
I send all down the flowering tree,
grandest tree in the cemetery.
The roots go deep into the clay,
to the brimstone where he must be.
Take it all, father, fill your arms,
like a sack. Take it with you.

I want bad memories out of my mind.
Take the numbness from my arms,
take the pain from my back,
take your terrible childhood,
take the disappointments of your father,
take your terror of death,
take your riddling cancer,
take your surly and curt ways,
all your sayings and platitudes,
your feelings that you couldn't get ahead,
your dirty, put-down, hatred jokes,

take all the times you said you were smarter,
the times you said I'd never be smart like you.
Take back, *You've been nothing but trouble*
since the day you were born,
and my mother waiting until your radio
program was over to deliver me.
Take back making it my fault your new shoes got ruined
when I was two and fell into the lake.
Take back believing you can draw better than I.
Take back believing I shouldn't go to college
and get *high-falutin'* ideas.
Take back, *You can't trust anyone but yourself.*
Take back all the times you mocked my mother
in front of company when you'd taken one too many drinks.
Take back your secret marriage to that show girl–
The secret you took to your grave,
 too ashamed to ever speak of it.

The roots are giant and deep. They travel miles
into the earth. Take all these things back. I confer them
on you, through the flowering Fig that Jesus cursed,
through your fear of god, they are yours. Take them.

Paint the Story

I

Faces buried in scarves and hats,
people cling to the Art Museum's
marble wall, to avoid the wind's whip.
Red noses protrude, glasses steam,
shoulders hunch like silver gray
pigeons on the sidewalk. A strange
young girl stands tall in a thin long
sleeved shirt. Her blond hair
braided in dreadlocks, her brow
furrowed, she appears unbothered
by the polar wind that torments
Chicago. Families surround small
children like penguins on an Antarctic
iceberg. Toes and faces pointed in,
they huddle for warmth. In a corner,
lovers are heating each other's lips.

A street person panhandles the crowd,
begs for dimes. Sweaters, jackets,
and coats layer his body. His fingers stick
out of shredded gloves, two hats cover
his head. To each refusal he replies:
I voted Republican. He stops to drink in
the crowd's humorous reaction, then
waits a moment to see if his comment
warrants a coin. Five minutes before noon,
an employee announces we can come in
out of the cold. A collective sigh of relief
sucks us through the revolving door.

My eyes look up the marble staircase,
gaze beyond the vaulted ceiling.
Voices echo and are swallowed in the air,
the same as in the great cathedrals of France.
Footsteps click on the floor. Parents tug
at children's coats, hush their laughter
of relief as they escape the cold. The museum
spirit pulls me up the stairs, breathes

life and feeling, speaks of beauty, stories
within, the heated passion of Gauguin's
south-sea oils, Van Gogh's gold and red
fire, the dance of life in Degas, flowers
in the painted garden of Monet.

II

Who needs French to read Lautrec?
He used no words to paint the story.
Those grand kicks at the Follies,
his mistress's face screams pain in green
off the corner of the painting.
I read that once she had been cut
from the picture. Which era couldn't
hold pain and joy in the same scene?
I look at her face; the way her lover
has painted her soul there. The kicks
of the Follies girls, disease and slovenliness
disguised in layers of tulle. The audience
drinks, talks, occasionally glances at the stage.
A man in a top hat, self portrait, smokes
a cigar. His lover screams off the canvas.

III

I made small-talk at a coffee shop
a month later, with the poet's husband,
a painter. I recalled that I always licked my
brushes to get a good point, particularly
useful for students with no funds for camel
hair. *Do you still paint*? he wondered.
When asked what medium he worked in,
he dropped a surprise. With a distant look,
he said, *Pastels, the closest to oils. Why do
you suppose all those painters were crazy?*
Brushes of lead poisoning whirled on their tongue.

First

Under "Jesus Knelt Praying on the Mount,"
my hair rolled up in curlers, Joe kisses me.

Jesus looks up to the sky, misses the kiss,
doesn't know this is the beginning

of everything. Warmth on my lips takes me
beyond paper curtains floating on the window,

worn arms, tears on the chair where we sit.
Who can think beyond his hand on my skin?

In the kitchen, Pa sits with a beer, ignores
Ma whining about food money not

in her purse. Eyes open wide, I watch us
walk into love. Even my fingers electrified

at the thought of leaving here. Attempting
to resist the heat between my legs, I've

lost command. Plunked crooked lamp
leans toward our warmth, the shade's

plastic ruffle curls up in passion. A bug-
eyed carnival cat considers our options,

his plaster chipped paws ready to pounce
on life. Gypsy lady ashtray looks the other

way, smirk on her face tells in a year Joe
will sit like pa with a beer and me, baby

on my hip griping about grocery money.
I practice writing Mrs. after Joe leaves.

Ignorant Bliss

There were days we screwed
in the morning before class,
met for lunch on the back stairs,
and again in the evening. We parked
anywhere between school and home.
Whenever I leave my car in the lot,
across from Wayne State's Old Main,
I remember I was once eighteen
and outrageously in love. I look
at the first car parked on the street
and see the old green Hudson.
I sat on top, navigated the depth
of penetration, mastered the rhythm.
Ignorant in the ways of men, I admire
his control more, as I age. How is it
possible? At this very moment, I feel
his cock moving in and out, that delicate
shaft strumming within. Insatiable,
naive, and stupid, for over a year,
on any street, two and three times
a day, in the woods on Belle Isle,
in parking lots, alleys, behind garages.
We defined fornication a new way,
agreed that as long as he didn't spend
in me, there was no mortal sin.
I practiced confession: *Father,*
I love sex. Father, It's wonderful.
Father, I'll do it again.

A Drop of Blood

But you, I beg you, don't be angry at her.
Each creature needs the help of every other.
-Bertolt Brecht

And if you're thirty, eighteen, or forty-two,
and if you've had sex only once this cycle
of the moon, whether you used a condom,
pill, diaphragm or god forbid
spontaneous sex, there are days when each
time you void, your finger reaches up to press
against the cervix, searching for pale pink,
red, yellow, albumen white, a sign your uterus
has not conceived. *On our lake, men go out,*
shake eggs in the nests of ducks and geese.

How many women have wept as they passed
their fetus at one month, two or more? Once,
you lost a child at five months; nurses could call
it a girl. You silently blessed her Susan,
too besieged to grieve, too tired to mind
the twelve month baby and pregnant again

the next month. Babies later, you cursed
your fertile body, stood on the basement
stairs, jumped from two, from four, from six,
tested your cervix, knew intuitively
about shaking eggs in the nest. Human
uterus, tougher than shell, the fetus grew.

Lit Fest on the Lawn; Homeless

For three days poets read, under a big white tent, on the Detroit Public Library lawn. We share a restroom with the homeless. One sits on the steps, clinging to a bag of nonsense, backpack weighing her shoulders, head hanging, nodding in the sun. A second bumps me as I enter the bathroom. I wonder, *Where do they go on Sundays when the library's closed?* In the middle of a reading, a short disheveled man sits right in front. His hair sticks out at angles, his balance awry, he swims dizzily in his single world. Agitated by microphoned cadence he walks up to the stage watching the poet, then leaves without being asked. Later, he returns, lays a wrapped Burger King on the seat next to him, sits with his arms and elbows between his legs, his head hanging down. When I ask him to leave, he never looks at me, never says a word, weaves out of the tent.

Up on stage, I notice he's back, sitting in my chair, eating my lunch. When the last poet is up on stage, when we're ready to pack unsold books, along comes Paul, 20 or 30, more able to blend into a crowd, unless you know what to look for. He wears a headband and a hat; an extra shirt hangs from his back pocket; his eyes have a glassy shine; at the edge of his mouth there's an inappropriate grin. If he wasn't black, I'd think he was my son. If his hair had some gray, I'd be confused. Not a poet, he's looking for a group he can join. I'm supposed to keep him out of my boss's hair. I ask him to pick up all the water bottles lying around, the lemonade cups, the straws, the napkins, the paper plates and plastic forks. Who would guess poets could be such slobs?

He works away, fills a box, returns. More like my grandson than a man, he offers it to me as a gift. I point to the trash can and say, *Put it there.* He is resting the box on his potbelly. It looks like my son's stomach, weight gain from twenty years of Lithium. In no time he's back, ready for more assignments. I send him to retrieve chairs that people have hauled out on the grass, to listen in a breeze. He folds up twenty-five and returns. My boss says, *Give him a five for a sandwich, I'll get the van.* Paul's eyes light up as I hand him money. I think of my son. I think of the shelter in San Francisco, the Salvation Army Captain in Dallas, jail in New Orleans. Paul doesn't leave; he thinks we're all his friends.

Hearing Bird Song, Shopping at Home Depot

Sparrows, small enough to creep
through ceiling cracks, slip into green
houses, so yesterday at Home Depot,
choosing flower boxes, dreaming
vibrant colors vining down, I wasn't
surprised to hear a robin's song
louder than life. Studying the garden-
center ceiling, I could not spot a bird.
Today, listening to Pattianne Rogers
read nature poetry, I realize the robin
song was counterfeit. I was tricked
by a clock, chimeless, from which
every hour a different bird song trills.
How is that different from listening to Rogers'
The Power of Toads, "calling and calling,
breeding/ Through a stormy evening
clasped atop their mates," her hummingbirds
being seduced by philosophical meaning,
her lover being compared to a deer,
a poppy, a boar snorgling and rooting.
But, these aren't metaphors. If she wants
to talk about sex, I wish she would.
April mornings, a cacophony of real
robins sing me awake. Leaning out
my window, I cheer on lusty courtships.

Chelonia

Crawling slowly across the street, wandering
from the lake—what could it have in mind?
Lifting the mud turtle away from my body
like a baby with soiled bottom, I'm an old
woman saving a turtle, as my daughters scream,
my sons-in-law laugh, my grandchildren stare in awe.
Every few seconds this green-shelled dead weight lets loose
some sort of rear end liquid. My grandson supposes
a kind of poison; he keeps his eye on the horned
toothless jaw. This animal trying to protect
itself, alternating between paddling his clawed
feet in the air and pulling all protrusions
into his shell. Leah, warily reaches her finger
up to touch the middle of the green black back.
Reaching the sand, shore of Walker Lake, I set
the bony shell, head, limbs and tail in water,
and the turtle swims away. What if it were
a female looking for a place to lay her eggs?
As with my adult children, the less I interfere
the better off we are. I remember a time
on Mio Pond: my brother and I capture
fifty baby turtles in a rowboat, he catches
flies, attempts to feed the hatchlings. I
dream up designs to paint on their backs, plan to sell
them back in Detroit, like a Kool-Ade stand:
Turtles 25¢. Mean, unreasonable
parents refuse to cooperate, insist we
dump them back in the pond. Haven't I learned,
isn't it time I realize, I can't rescue
anything. I can't make life *right.* It's time to retire
each night without going over offsprings' names
and lives, picturing them happy, satisfied,
safe. I nod off on the back of a tortoise tall
as an elephant. I'm grabbing the air, slipping
over the edge, looking for some way to hold on.

Shadows

Now that he's a shadow on the horizon,
the distance is like a cool cloth on my rage.
His silhouette's buried in a shoebox
of photos shipped from Florida after Mother
died. Not easy to open that crate packed
the same day as her funeral. Eyes shut,
I reach in, feel for the cardboard box we sifted
through as we sat on her bed, pictures bridging
their lifetimes. Mother in beaver coat,
me not born. Pictures of my infants, lost

to children who carried their baby books away
as they grew. A color photograph, faded brown
and gray–my phantom father holds a ship rail, pauses–
he is a sepia silhouette, next to a blazing
sunset. In my mind, he is one with day's end,
the distance between his life and mine lengthening
like his shadow in the failing sun. I think
of him in terms of decades, now that he is just
a trace. He was only thirty when I fell nose
down in the water. With new shoes on he lifts

my two-year-old body out, then at seventy
he complains of ruined shoes. Since he's faded
to a shadow, I study this next picture, slim man
in his fifties posing at the farm with my two daughters,
not capable of touch or hug. Summer, my girls,
five and three, stand in panties, but he is more
pathetic, hot. He cuts acres of grass each weekend,
pushes the lawn mower when the thermometer edges
on 103. He stands in his ancient bathing suit,

possibly blue, a rubberized knit that's lost
elasticity, hanging loose from his waist.
Father's penis and testicles suspended in
the tired folds like a ballet dancer. Hands stiffly
held by his side. Shadow on the horizon, distance

lets me say, *father's penis, bony knees, narrow
feet.* Thin musculature in his arms, no clue
of cancer or pain in his blue eyes still, lack
of gut, a sign he worked hard, not back to drink
yet. Look back at the ship-rail stance, his stomach
protrudes. Ten acres on Hayes Road in Michigan,
bought after the war, gave him plenty to do
weekends besides drink. Sunday afternoons before
then, Mother warns us not to wake the sleeping
demon hungover on the couch. Did he buy
the acres on the Clinton River to save a marriage,
or for my brothers and me, almost a teen, resenting
the hour drive away from the flat in Detroit,
away from my friends. And anyway, don't I
remember that fight late at night, when Mother

gave her ultimatum, *Stop drinking or I...*
Now Father's shadow is near sunset; a sunset
that slips off glossy paper. I see a smile on
his face. Mother snapped the pictures, his eyes
as he stands between two grandchildren are like
Hank Williams singing, "Have I told you lately -
that I love you?" Bony ribs, he wore sleeveless
undershirts, boxer shorts; once at midnight. I opened
my bedroom door to Father, two feet away, heading

for the bathroom, shorts clutched in his hands, knobby
flank of bare hip. He's calling, *Edna, Edna, get out
here.* Smoothing her nightgown, actually pulling it
on, pushing me back to bed. He thought he was
a failure all his life. Now ingrained in my brain,
he's a sunset glowing off glossy paper, still always
cloudy, a sepia shade pulled down over memory.

Blue

Blue, titian blue Morning Glories climb, fill my trellis,
overflow themselves. He says, *"Now we are in trouble,"*

picks the ovum, splits the cover to expose four seeds.
My heart lifts; what is it that gives me this joy? He says

seriously, *"Morning Glory will be everywhere – there is
nothing we can do."* Yes, this is good, this is good.

The seed comes genetically set. I can water, feed, train it
up the trellis. Some seeds wither, some come misformed,

some have a kink that won't allow regeneration. Seed
exposed on stone is not able to lift to blue. Beauty of blue

flows over my sorrow, son who never learned from us
to treat his wife so poorly. Unlike his father who nourishes

my life with touch and kiss, kind word, fine meals
and understanding. But he, the father, frowns

at Morning Glory doing what is expected, swirling,
lifting blooming hundreds of cerulean, cobalt, azure,

aqua, bice – any of a group of colors that may vary
in lightness and saturation – whose hue is that of a clear

sky; the hue of that portion of the spectrum lying between
green and violet; evoked in the normal observer

by radiant energy of wavelength approximately
four-hundred-seventy-five nanometers,

a small blue butterfly of the family Lycaenidae,
the blue whole in the morning sunlight.

Whales Weep Not

-D.H. Lawrence

Sitting in a deck chair,
out on the Pacific,
eighty miles from shore–watch
>   *Promise me–promise– you'll never put me*
>   *in a nursing-home– while I'm in my right mind.*
nine humpbacks gambol,
throw their spouts up,
lift their backs,
>   The shatter of life's end approaches, this exquisite
>   moment swells, the potential of death compounds awe.
the dorsal fin so clear
against the glimmering
sunglinted ocean.
>   This intense view pierces me. *Who are you?*
>   *Not my daughter.* A shadow of mother persistent
>   in the mind's bay thrust up in the whale's sea mist.
The elongated "ohhh"
of my shipmates
as each whale flips his tail
at the sky. As they dive
and surf, leap through the air.
>   Wondering if mother still lives, my stomach seizes
>   in pain, relives signing nursing-home papers.
The snow-covered mountains,
this far out to sea,
disappear on the horizon
in a fury of sunset.
>   *Bury me in my pink gown; I'll glide*
>   *into the unknown, my twisted legs free.*

IV. Passage

The past is but the beginning of a beginning, and all that is and has been is but the twilight of the dawn.
                                    -Herbert George Wells

let fall come

let the wind blow

we have steeped
in summer

sucked the beauty
of our gardens

treasured their color
then let fall come

Stunned

for Stellasue

We sit on a yellow bench
listen to Lake Walloon waves
lap, the gasp of cold
from a young swimmer...

I'm convinced we're all dancing
 as fast as we can, she says.
Look at us getting old. What
do we have left, twenty years?

Her hair caught in sunshine wisp,
eyes innocent as blue,
my mind sees her heart
heave her translucent chest,
All I know is my truth,
she murmurs.   Stunned.

Her man lies alone in ICU,
blood clots in his heart.
He sent her north saying,
Nothing you can do, nothing.
What grips the Autumn
breeze is how she accepts
the parameters, full wisdom of pain.

Two of us, legs outstretched
in late September sun, *Have him*
take the treatment that gives
the least side effects, buy twelve
years, she says of my husband's
cancer. *This is no time to have*
a pity part; it's time to act.

We're all dancing.

Cold Marble

Sitting on the steps of Rome's Metro,
a gypsy woman cradles her sleeping toddler.
Eyes out of focus, stringy hair, raggedy clothes,
she seems old – might be thirty-three. A basket,
a sign in English: *I have no home, no bed,*
no food for the bambino, Please.

I've heard of the man who felt another's hand
in his pants pocket pilfering his wallet.
I haven't seen the older gypsy, two bags
in her arms, brush against American tourists
as a child slips below the sacks, empties
travelers' fanny packs. I'm on my way
to the coliseum, huge stone and timber structure
where Romans watched slaves
tear each other to shreds,

when I drop a few coins in her basket.
No recognition on the mother's face;
the child sleeps on. I won't believe
gypsies want to sit on cold marble
Metro steps begging for lire
as throngs rush by.
When I was thirty-three,
I said I'd scrub toilets
to feed my kids. If I
were Egyptian we'd be sisters.
It was just a few coins.

Distractions

To Everything There is a Season
Ecclesiastes 32

I

His wings a quiet motor, air so still
I hear the thrum of a hummingbird's wings
as he slips his elongated beak
into one of the feeders.
There's the mallard in my flower garden;
he keeps one plant mowed
to the ground. Each day, he returns
to clip back the small bit of growth.
Me not even sure what grows there.
This morning a strange procession,
thirteen ducks walk out from the lake,
through our back yard, single file pass up
seed on the ground under the birdfeeder,
march over the hill. It's the middle of August
and I don't know what they're doing
or why they're doing it. So far this morning,
I've seen chickadees, cardinals, crows, house finches,
one ruby-throated hummingbird, and a swallowtail.
It must be a sign of old age to watch the birds. A poet
friend thinks it's my obsession.

II

Later today, the phone will ring. It will be
Jim's doctor telling him his PSA is up,
giving him the name of a urologist, urging him
to get a biopsy. My sweet love's face will go gray
but the children are over for some birthday
celebration and he wants to shield them
and shield himself. He hates pity
and they do see us as ancient folk,
possibilities of being a problem or a chore to them.
Oh, I don't mean they don't love us. It's just
they're in the middle of building their lives
and we, we've lifted the last Lego to the top of the tower,
intend to enjoy the view. Not in a sedentary way,
isn't it true if the young have left the nest,

life is no longer work nine to five, isn't it time
to enjoy, to travel, see a bit of the world?

III

It took two months to get here: here going back
to the surgeon that will remove his prostate.
Here past the fear, the anger, the rage, somewhere
in the middle of acceptance. In this sorrow, in this
change, I notice we each reach out more often,
with a tenderness, with an outward sign of love.
It is as if this "it," cancer, moves us closer to oneness.
Have you noticed in Autumn the birds change?
The juncos are back, not a single hummingbird
in weeks. Woodpeckers in herringbone suits fly
in for suet, Blue jays are thrashing and feisty,
chickadees stuff themselves with sunflower seed.
Soon snow and cardinals will appear. Tomorrow
the surgeon's appointment in the same hospital
that has nurtured our premature granddaughter,
Erin, who came home yesterday.
Her parents waited six weeks.
I haven't seen a robin since May.

Asteroid May or May Not Hit Earth in 2019

Newspaper headline 2002

Astronomers debate whether a space rock
will crash on our planet in seventeen years.
A Cambridge sky gazer says, *Don't sweat it.*

The picture in my newspaper depicts
the epicenter, with an arrow, right over
my house. Do you suppose the *New York*

Times moves the arrow over to their state?
In 2019, I won't be quite ninety years old.
I might be walking to my mailbox

when the asteroid arrives. Total destruction
is predicted for the 150-mile center.
On the other hand, temperatures

will drop 45 degrees on the other side
of Earth. If it's January in Russia,
it'll get pretty cold. Last night,

my neighbor ran down to the lake
in her bathrobe. Her 85 year-old husband
had decided to spread mole poison while

she showered and had fallen and lay unnoticed
on the beach for twenty minutes. When EMS
finally came he refused to go to the hospital.

Do you suppose young people worry
more about asteroids or being responsible
for aging parents? If the arrow belongs

where the *Free Press* put it, *no problemo.*

Point of View

After surgery, catheter in place,
bloody urine bag clipped to the bedside,
you lie eviscerated, eyes closed.

Our daughters sit with me, stare at you
in bed. The bag fills with blood, blood
of your body. I think of the inferno

in your eyes during frantic love-making
these past weeks. *This can't be happening
to us,* you murmured in my arms. Jenny

flips pages of *Better Homes and Garden.*
Here, her sister points out a kitchen sink.
During the four-hour surgery, Annie says,

Father must live. He will be all right.
My heart pummels my ribs. The surgeon
stops by, speaks in cliché.

*It was encapsulated; we got it all. You can
go home tomorrow.* Your turned head stares
at the wall, at the white sterile nothing.

I stand by the bed, squeeze your hand, bite
my lip, try to erase my mind's eye view of you
poised over me in passion. Months after,

at night in bed, you murmur, *If I had it
to do over, I'd never have the surgery.*
The children went home relieved.

Letter to Memory

It pains me that you hide so much. I search
within to find you. Your shape not like the contour
of the heart or brain, like noodles pressed
inside the skull. Yet, you're there somewhere.

As time passes, you've become stingy, unwilling
to let go of song titles, book characters, phone
numbers, old friends' names and dates. But you
embarrass me, calling out *Hello* to son Tom,
when you realize full well I am speaking to David.

Lately, you've been visiting my dreams, images
from years ago, identifying a grandson's birth
with my multiple deliveries, rushing from this
daughter's birth, to a son born forty years ago.
And it hardly seems fair to bring up old lovemaking
in my sleep. But do you help with who's had Measles
or Scarlet Fever? While my body's gained weight
with age, you've become anorectic. So sparse you
spill no beans before third grade. Fortunately,

you seem to have lost 90% of the horror of a first
marriage. Please, could you hold on to these last
twenty-five years, at least the very best parts?
What is the point of trekking through Italy
if one can't savor the view over Sorrento,
wander through back streets in Florence? Feel
again the smooth blue silk scarves in the market.
I wonder what color you are. I know you can smell.
Send scents of lavender from Mother's handkerchief
drawer. Help me remember the touch of her hand,
my baby's hair, the pulse in the fontanel of grandchildren,
a pine needle bed in the woods one night.

Death-Defying Wrinkles

*...because we are transformed by what we flee
and have no say, who are in flight.*
                    -Mark Halperin

My mother died at ninety-six. The week before,
I'm lifting her from the wheelchair, helping her
to the toilet. Pausing to rest, gripping the sink,
staring into the bathroom mirror,
she says, *I look like an old lady.*

She opens the medicine cabinet, reaches
for lipstick and motions for me to color
her lips, says, *That's better,* fluffs the front
of her hair. Every two years or so,
I'm suckered in by some age-defying make up.

Toner, conditioner, mask or cream, I use them
once, see no difference in my mirror, only more
of her. Eyeliner falls from the cabinet each time
I open the door, I sweep bottles and jars
up and throw them in the trash. Mirrors lie more

than memory. Memory lies. Looking in mirrors,
catching my reflection in a window, running
to catch a plane, I almost run into a white-haired
lady. That nanosecond when the mind flashes
faster than the speed of light and suddenly I realize,

My god, that's me. Run fingers over face, forehead,
nose, feel my hair, shoulder length – no – cut short
these many years. Rising from a family room chair,
photos on the wall, all those daughters more me
than I am. My eyes on one, nose over there, the next

speaks with my voice. I am lost, becoming
extinct, becoming my dead mother. I should
have been dropping string behind me like
the Botanist in Africa measuring how far

I had come through the forest of my life. My feet
are far enough from my eyes; there is no sign
of their age. My hands are mother's hands,
puckered. What would be the point of a face lift
without a neck tuck, and then layer by layer
a shrinking of the skin that gloves the twenty-six
bones in my hand, which, I'm told, death does
on its own. I'm off to see my brother for the first
time since she died. I bet he'll catch me in the corner
of his eye, think I'm Edna come back to life.

Body Parts, Forefingers

Caesar sits on a stone throne in the Coliseum,
drinks iced Lipton tea. His lizard tongue flicks
down the sides of the goblet, catches skin of lemon,
shards of ice, rolls over ruby-crusted lip of cup.

His servant serving tea has a slight case
of Tourette's, whispers, *Lizard lips, forked tongue,*
(father holds the Tobia's cock for you good price,)
poisonous flicker, flicker, flick, flack, fuck, fuck.

Five maiden servants stand 'round Caesar, fan
him with palm leaves, lift the fronds up
and down; their eyes and groins rivet on slaves
below who grease each others' biceps,

strip down to loin clothes, raise penetrating eyes
to their Ruler's box, lock on the breathless
maiden breasts protruding from summer gauze,
members lift to life as they ready for their demise.

Romans in the stands clack chicken bones, used
as tickets, against the stone benches sounding
like a giant coffee grinder. Weary of waiting
for the next issue of wild beasts, their eyes drool

at the thought of more slaves relieved of arms
and legs, a chaw from a belly. Outside the arena
one clever tradesman has set up a stand selling
body parts from public statues around Rome,

treasured souvenirs to take home to the family.
Hidden beneath his kiosk there's a bag of particular
parts, the cock of Tobias, breast of Maid Mary,
a dragon's thigh bone, forefingers from five dead

popes. These will go to the highest bidder, he who
offers the most gold coin imprinted with the current
Caesar's silhouette, tête-à-tête pieces for future
feasts served at their estate. *Lizard lips, forked*

tongue, the tradesman's son comes by Tourette's
naturally, lifts his hand holding a small bag of coins,
waves to his father as he descends carved stone steps,
smiles at his sale, body parts, *flicker, flick, fuck, feast.*

I Listen to Ghosts

I want you to know Mother stands
over by my sink – she never sat down –
peels potatoes, shakes her head
at my family today. I suppose
Mother thinks there's something
I should do. Our daughter will marry
in Chicago. Our daughter lives in sin.
Whoever heard of such a thing?
Watch Mother shake her head,
make a sign of the cross
with her potato-wet fingers,
touch her temple, look up to heaven,
a bit of brown skin caught on her brow.
What kind of priest marries these
children who've been living in sin?
It was never like this in my day.

It occurs to me, Mother married
at 29, the same age as our daughter.
She has lots to say about my children,
but never speaks of her wedding.
I consider asking if a virgin
stood before the Justice of the Peace.
But then, she drones on, *White*
is for purity, points the potato peeler

at me. Look at me, sixty-seven, I sit
in this kitchen chair like a six-year-old
and now Father pipes in, *This is your*
Mother's wedding. And it's 1955,
I'm twenty-one, and he means she will make
all the decisions. I won't be able
to sew my bridal dress. Don't you
wonder how many ghosts walk
in one kitchen? I look again at Mother
and think, *Times are different.*
Let's stop with the questions already.

Island Crags

Every time my bladder badgers me in Italy, it takes
fifteen-hundred lire, a quarter American to use filthy
or spotlessly clean latrines. Walking Isle of Capri's stone-clad shore,

waiting for the boat to Sorrento, I find the world-wide symbol,
stick-figure men and women. Outside the door, a gypsy girl
hunches up on her knees begging; cardboard sign in English

says she has no home. In the dim shadow, not one but three
harridans sit on tattered folding chairs, legs akimbo, wary eyes
peering from the cave, dark noxious hall outside the convenience.

A team, two motion to a basket in the third's lap. My coin clanks
against others; they point to the seatless toilet, filthy floor, lack
of paper, stench. Using peddler's Kleenex, I stare at rust stains

stretched down the sink to its drain, the constant drip here
in the underbelly of Capri, island of five-star hotels, gold bracelets
and gelato. Hips wide with pasta, shoes run down, henna hair,

chapped hands, wrinkled cheeks, ragged sweaters, aprons over black,
arms folded against need, where do these grandmothers gathering
coins from the *turista* live? Their hoard of lire won't get them a boat

ride back to Sorrento. I can't afford more than gelato or a glass of wine
on scenic Capri. Sky indigo, shimmering bay, the town hangs
from sides of the island's crags. Tell me, where do these women go?

Filling in the Blanks

Without our personal memories, we fall victim
entirely to the terror of the vanished past.
                                    -Gregory Orr

It was one day this week, I realized, in the course
of making order from the chaos of two children's lives,
I've lost chunks of remembrance of my others growing up.

Certainly, I recall my firstborn's first step, first word,
first brilliance in school. My mind attempts balance
against the horror of his teen years. I fall asleep nights
squaring up his small successes, counting his coup as if

it were my own. Little record is left of later children's
beginnings. In fact, I find myself obsessing–searching through
my ill-filled recollections, poking scanty parts of my brain
for visions of their childhood. Silently, I ask forgiveness,
wish I could recollect more. I grasp for sweet pictures:
a quiet walk around the block, two squeezed in a stroller,

one holding on, two ahead on tricycles. Now, brave daughters,
bearing children, call me for advice or to report a child's
accomplishment, filling in the blanks of my vanished past.

Yesterday, as I nuzzled the youngest's black hair, her mother,
happiness glistening in her eyes, said, *Now that I have*
a daughter of my own, I realize how much you loved me.

Small Bursts of Beauty

Standing in the Opera House
parking lot, lights
from Comerica Park
glisten on shards of glass
hanging from windows
in the abandoned top
five floors of the Harmonie
House Bar and Grill.
The featured poets
from Anchorage and New York
have left for the St. Regis Hotel,
tired old lady
on Grand Boulevard.
Alone by my car,
I reckon with
small bursts of beauty
in the city,
balance glass shards
and poets introduced
against the landscape
of a new baseball diamond,
married to the Michigan
Opera house.
The trick is not to give
up on the city, not
to give up on its people.
I nod goodnight
to sparkling glass,
imagine a brighter
heart of this Detroit City:
Woodward Avenue mimicking
the shopping streets of Budapest,
an underground rail as timely
as Rome's, an audience
for poetry as large as those
found in Comerica Park.

Salt

In the end one of us will need to remember this.
    - Li-Young Lee

I count the shimmers like holy water,
drops of urine sparkle on the head of your penis,
your salt mixes with my salt-fed tears
as I lift your soft piece to my mouth in prayer.
Prayer that one day nerves will heal
and you will lift and enter me again.

I'll take you in; you on top, watching your mouth,
your face. Or from behind, like a loveknot,
turn and watch you. Later, lovemaking over,
we'll lie, silently weep, as we did those weeks
before your surgery. Every day realizing,
it may be the last of joylove this way.

So now, after a time of hopeful practice,
when you find your shorts soaked, my heart
springs, envelops you with the passion you've
showered on me for years. I must find peace
in my heart, enough to forgive the gods
that struck, collapsed our tent. Together
our necessity urges us to build a fresh shelter.

Woman Grows Old

Maybe it is time for me to practice
growing old.
                    -Stanley Kunitz

I

Walking in Lucca in the pouring
rain I hear my mother, *You'll catch cold.*
Doctors claim it's not true.

Walking in Lucca in the pouring rain
I begin to cough. Ten days later,
the doctor says pneumonia.

The kitchen floor was clean the day
we left. Today, my weak hand
drops a pill. It rests in a cobweb

hammock. My fingers tangle in the silk,
struggle to free the medicine.
Determination of an unthwarted spider

rings in my mind with my husband's voice,
It takes longer to recover
at your age. Snow on the ground.

II

Some things hard to look at, the black
hair above my lip I could pluck with closed
eyes. Why do I love you more when we're

alone? Ted Turner's wife left him; felt
she'd lost her voice in the relationship.
I think some things aren't worth arguing

about; resentment builds like snow
compressed until it won't be broken up.
Our difference is an olive seed in the pit

of my stomach. Which parts of the whole
can I live with–love–hate? Which
repels me more, my double chin

or yours? I hear leaves crackle and fall
outside our window. Sun as far south
in the sky as it can go; evening chilled

as a knee ache. Tree branches reach
nakedness to January blue,
leaves piled in my garden

cover bulb roots and mother's ashes.
Rust Sedum and stalks of Cone flower
shadow the snow-filled yard.

III

Blind, he fumbled at furniture to move from living room
to toilet. Grandpa wore the same baggy gray pants held up
by suspenders, long-sleeved underwear beneath a blue-striped
cotton shirt. He kept a pack of squared toilet paper in his right
pant pocket, every few minutes he spit phlegm in a square,
wrapped and placed it in his left pocket. Smelling of musty
mold and green moss, every ten minutes he'd hack a huge
hocking cough. Sitting in the living room arm-chair, the one
nobody sat in it was so uncomfortable, bent head to a small
radio, ear touching the brown fabric smelling of burned wire,
speaker turned low. At supper, food stuck in his mustache,
fell on his chest. After I put my pj's on, mother would say,
Kiss Grandpa goodnight. His cheeks and chin were prickly
sharp, the musk of long-worn clothing offended my nose.
Seeming not to know my name, he'd pat my hand, smile a bit.
I knew him for two weeks; he returned to Washburn, WI,
to the boarding house. Rocked on the porch in the summer,
winter sat in his room, ear to his radio, a gray blanket around
his shoulders to ward off draft. He died at sixty-five.

IV

I see her younger now, my mother–
a reflection in the doorwall glass.
I don't believe in ghosts. Do I?

She stands in my bathrobe, watches me.
And then there is a cramp or something
in my chest, near my heart.
I should call her; it's Saturday.
Monday, the last red leaves drop,
I remember she's not here.

The Dance of the Horses: *La Danza de los Corceles*

We lie in separate beds in the dark. Below our window, some drunks
sing at a bar, mask sobbing tears cascading down cheeks.
In the morning, I look in the mirror of the marble walled Spanish

bathroom and see not a bridge, cathedral, or mosque, but a desolate
woman. Hopeless. That day we travel to Jerez to an equestrian show,
dancing stallions, their manes trailing in the air like wind-swept

willow branches. Bulging black eyes look out from lashes curled like a
strumpet's. If a horse dare lift his head, the rider pulls tight
on the rein. My chest heaves as hoofs clop in measured cadence.

Forced to walk lifted steps, head bowed, front feet high, bit in
their mouths, like your disease, strangling. Saliva slathers over the
steel. I am crying for the horse, for you. A rider forces the largest

stallion up on hind feet. Ordered to jump, he snorts in effort. Half
a ton of horse lifts off the sand-covered arena, over and over, again
and again in *Corbeta,* powerless to do anything but obey. His

colossal cock and balls sway uselessly in front of him. Just then
a group of four horses pulling a carriage enters the arena, whipped,
harnessed, controlled. There in front, a stallion rebels at his bit,

lifts up out of measure, tries to loose himself of the reins, and falls,
swipes at his partner; huge horses tumble tangled in legs and gear,
drivers run about shouting; using whips. Embarrassed, they've lost

control before an audience of two thousand. The trainer, a young
man, leaps from the stands, runs to his fallen horse, pounds
his rump, calls for him to rise, and I recognize the call.

Watching the horse struggle to his feet, I weep. That night
when I crawl into bed, you whisper, *I miss touching you.* We find each
other's bodies beneath the twists and turns of the sheets.

Acknowledgments

Grateful acknowledgment to the editors of the following journals and anthologies in which some of these poems, or earlier versions of them, first appeared:

Clackamas (2002): "At Ten I Was a Boy, Sometimes."
Diner (Spring/Summer 2001): "Waiting for the Taxi to the Airport on the Way to the Nursing Home in Michigan.
Driftwood Review (2000): "Nightwatch" ; *Graffiti Rag* (1995): "The Last Night"; *Graffiti Rag* (1998): "Pulse."
Heartlands Today; Midwest Sirens and Muses Volume 8: "Smooth Sidewalks"; *Heartlands Today; Midwest Characters & Voices,* Volume 9: "I Was a Pool Shark at the Jefferson Avenue YMCA"
Moxie; The Body Eclectic: "Do It To Me One More Time."
Now Here Nowhere Volume 2, # 1: "Bulemic" (title "What Shall I Say Because Talk I Must"); *Now Here Nowhere* Volume 2, # 3: "Matchbook Love," and "I Want My Mother"; *Now Here Nowhere* Volume 2, #4: "King of My World."
#Sharp: "Do It To Me One More Time."
Sweet Annie Review: About Him: "Dance Naked."
The MacGuffin, Volume XV Number 3: "Visiting Hour"; *The MacGuffin* Volume XVIII, Number 2, "Island Crags"; *The MacGuffin, Volume XIX,* Number 1: "Nests", and "I Count Them Over, Every One Apart, My Rosary, My Rosary" (title "Pass On").
The Paterson Review, Volume VIII: "Throat" and "Too Far" (title "Breath"); *The Paterson Review,* Volume 31: "Drop of Blood" and "Woman Growing Old."
Potpourri: National Poetry Award lst Prize 2001: "Until the Stitches Come Out."
Rattapallax Press: Dialogue Through Poetry (2001): "Chelonia."
Rattle Number XV: "Lit Fest on the Lawn; Homeless."
The Touchstone Journal 2001: "Mason City Ladies Sewing Circle," MFA Graduate First Prize.
Tyme Gallery: "Never Say Never," Honorable Mention 2001.
Woman Spirit: Sustaining Voices: "Pulse."
"Smooth Sidewalks" was included in *Century of Voices* (Detroit Women Writers, 1999).
"I Was a Poolshark at the Jefferson Avenue YMCA" was included in *Abandon Automobile,* an anthology published by Wayne State University Press, 2001.
"Pulse" won second place in the national *Art in the Air* Poetry contest 2001.
"Throat" received Honorable Mention in the 14th Annual *Paul Laurence Dunbar Poetry Contest, 2000.*
"A Drop of Blood" received 3rd Place from *AMP Arts: Austin's Magazine of Progressive Art,2001.*

Mary Ann Wehler was born and raised in Detroit, Michigan. She taught for 30 years, then earned her MFA degree in Poetry from Vermont College. She is Assistant to the Director of Detroit's The Writer's Voice and editor of their newsletter. She also serves as Poet in Residence at the Troy Public Library in Michigan where she has taught creative writing for the last four years and at the Detroit Opera House. She believes strongy in the truth, peace, and joy to be found in writing. Her first book of poems was *Walking Through Deep Snow* (Plain View Press 1997). Her work also has appeared in *The Patterson Review, The McGuffin Reader, Rattle,* and in *Variations of the Ordinary: A Woman's Reader* (Plain View Press, 1955).